ABSOLUTE BEGINNERS
Electronic Drums

Written by Noam Lederman
Edited by David Bradley and Adrian Hopkins
Music processed by Paul Ewers Music Design
Book design by Chloë Alexander
Photography by Matthew Ward
Pages 5 & 7 photos courtesy of Getty Images

Music recorded, mixed and
mastered by Jonas Persson
Electronic drums by Noam Lederman
Backing tracks by Jonas Persson
Bass guitar by Tom Farncombe
Additional guitar by Adrian Hopkins

www.noamlederman.com
www.vvinner.com

Noam plays Mapex drums, Paiste cymbals, and Vic Firth sticks.

Special thanks to Emilie Birks and Gavin Thomas at Yamaha.

PLAYBACK+
Speed • Pitch • Balance • Loop

To access audio, visit:
www.halleonard.com/mylibrary

Enter Code
5101-0761-6919-5775

ISBN 978-1-78305-848-8

World headquarters, contact:
Hal Leonard
7777 West Bluemound Road
Milwaukee, WI 53213
Email: info@halleonard.com

In Europe, contact:
Hal Leonard Europe Limited
Dettingen Way
Bury St Edmunds, Suffolk, IP33 3YB
Email: info@halleonardeurope.com

In Australia, contact:
Hal Leonard Australia Pty. Ltd.
4 Lentara Court
Cheltenham, Victoria, 3192 Australia
Email: info@halleonard.com.au

HAL•LEONARD®

Visit Hal Leonard Online at **www.halleonard.com**

Explore the entire family of Hal Leonard products and resources

SHEET MUSIC DIRECT   SheetMusicPlus   HAL LEONARD'S ESSENTIAL ELEMENTS **music class**    ESSENTIAL ELEMENTS *Interactive*

 ArrangeMe®   n o t e f l i g h t   groove3    musicroom

Contents

Introduction

Welcome to *Absolute Beginners Electronic Drums*.

This book is designed for anyone that wants to play the electronic drums. By working through the book you will learn how to perform grooves and fills in various styles, from rock to metal, and from hip hop to funk. To help you learn, backing tracks to play along with in each style are provided in this book.

We have also included a recommended listening guide for each one of the styles, which we hope you will find inspirational.

Playing an electronic drum kit is similar in many ways to playing an acoustic drum kit. However, there are advantages and disadvantages for each instrument (see page 6) and it is important that you are aware of those in order to achieve whatever goals you set for yourself. The good news is that with minimal adjustments you will be able to play both types of kits using the same techniques learned here.

The fundamentals of music notation and basic techniques are explained in detail to allow you to get playing straight away. So, grab your sticks and let's do it!

The first electronic drum is said to have been created by Graeme Edge, drummer for The Moody Blues, and Professor Brian Groves in 1971. It was later used in the song 'Procession' from *Every Good Boy Deserves Favour* by The Moody Blues that was released that year. The next significant development happened in 1981 when the electronic drum company Simmons released its first commercial electronic drum kit, the SDS-V.

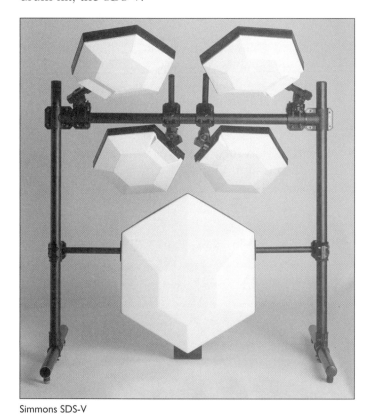

Simmons SDS-V

This product attracted the attention of many professional drummers at the time, some of whom decided to experiment and integrate the electronic drum kit into their setup and music. If you listen to any Duran Duran or Rush album from the early 1980s and hear an electronic snare drum, you are probably listening to the famous Simmons electronic snare sound.

Simmons' success was limited, however, and new companies in the market began to develop advanced products that attracted many drummers worldwide. Over the years, the companies Yamaha and Roland became the leaders in the field of electronic drums. They constantly pushed the boundaries of what was possible and what could be achieved with electronic drums.

Currently the leading products are the Yamaha DTX 950K and the Roland TD-30KV. These electronic drum kits offer high quality digital sounds, realistic hi-hats and drumheads, and much more.

It seems that the development of the electronic drum kit is not complete, but has only just begun, and with the advancement of technology the possibilities are limitless. It is exciting to see what the future holds for this instrument.

Graeme Edge (The Moody Blues)

Neil Peart (Rush)

Roger Taylor (Duran Duran)

Electronic versus Acoustic

If you have bought this book and already own an electronic drum kit, then you have made your decision. However, it is important to be aware of the advantages and disadvantages of the electronic drum kit when compared to the traditional acoustic kit.

The disadvantages of the electronic kit:
* Electronic kits are largely more expensive, especially the top models which offer the most desirable technology.

* An electronic kit will always need a mains power source and amplification.

* The sound produced is not exactly the same as acoustic drums (if you start on an electronic kit this will not necessarily be a problem).

The advantages of the electronic kit:
* Electronic kits take up less space.

* Sound levels of electronic kits are more easily controlled.

* Electronic kits can be used with headphones.

* Most models have a metronome built in as well as play-along song tracks.

* Electronic drums can be recorded directly without needing any microphones.

* You can easily connect an audio device to play along with your favourite music.

* Electronic kits incur less wear and tear on drumheads and drumsticks compared to acoustic kits.

Yamaha Stage Custom

VS

Yamaha DTX562K

The top three leaders in the market of electronic drum kits are Yamaha, Roland, and Alesis. However, every year there are more than a few new brands that try to join the electronic drum kit race and offer similar (or better) technology for a cheaper price. Therefore, it is crucial that you do your research before buying. Read reviews from other users as the price is not the most important parameter for buying an instrument.

You want to buy an instrument that will be durable, produce good sounds, and will be fun to play. Set a budget and find the best electronic drum kit in the market that suits your needs.

Generally speaking, with electronic drum kits the more you pay the better technology, quality of sounds, and amount of options you will have. So it really depends how often you will be using the kit. Will you be gigging with it or only playing for fun at home? How important is the sound quality to you?

A trip to your local music shop is much recommended. This way you can not only learn about the differences between the kits, but also try to play them and see what feels right to you. Your local music shop will also be able to provide you with a warranty from the manufacturer and assist in case something goes wrong.

Roland TD-4KP Drums

Alesis DM7 Kit

The Electronic Drum Kit

There are many different electronic drum kits available to the beginning player and each one has its unique features and possible setups. However, the basic electronic drum kit setup is exactly the same as the basic acoustic drum kit setup. It consists of pads that are clamped to a frame (or rack) to resemble a bass drum, snare drum, two rack toms, floor tom, a hi-hat, ride cymbal, and crash cymbal. There may be a slight variation from kit to kit; there maybe another floor tom or cymbal in the high-end kits.

The size of the drums and cymbals does not affect the sound as it is an electronic sound that you are triggering. Therefore, even if you wanted a big rock sound from the drums, you do not need to opt for a kit with large pads; you'd need to select a 'Rock' kit from the list of preset kits stored in the module (or 'brain'). Do make sure that whatever kit you choose, it fits the room you are going to place the kit in.

Drum Pads

Also known as *triggers*, these pads are synthetic playing surfaces that are shaped like small drums or practice pads. In this traditional setup, each drum pad will trigger one sound from the acoustic drum kit. The pad sizes vary from brand to brand but do not affect the sound in any way.

Trigger pads are largely made from rubber, mesh, and silicone. The cheapest and most basic pads are made from rubber and offer limited bounce (or rebound) than the more advanced pads made from mesh and silicone.

A TCS (textured cellular silicone) one-zone pad, the XP70

These are newer technologies that offer much better rebound and a more natural feel than the older rubber pads. Therefore, if you can only afford to buy one trigger pad made from silicone, use it as your snare drum.

A three-zone pad (with pad controller), the XP120SD

Cymbal Pads

The same concept applies to cymbal pads. These are generally round or triangular in shape and made out of rubber.

A one-zone pad, the TP70

The PCY135

Playing Zones

Every pad offers up to three playing zones. This means that you can achieve three different sounds from hitting different zones of the pad. This will be extremely useful as you develop and want the ability to play a variety of sounds from each pad, exactly like an acoustic drum kit. If you want to read more about the sound possibilities, see page 13 in this book, 'Changing Sounds'.

Setting Up Your Kit

1 Assembling the rack

Every electronic kit comes with a rack. This is the frame of the kit and all the trigger pads will be mounted to it. These are usually very easy to assemble—just follow the instructions from the manufacturer. Make certain you are near to a power source (see **8**).

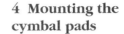

2 Mounting the drum pads

Start with the snare drum then follow with the hi tom, medium tom and floor tom. Ensure that you can easily reach each drum and everything feels comfortable.

3 Position the drum throne

Set the drum throne to a comfortable height and check the positions of the drum pads again. Adjust if necessary.

4 Mounting the cymbal pads

The cymbal pads locks will look slightly different to the drum pads. However, the concept is the same. Ensure that the pads are fully secured and easily accessible before moving to the next stage.

5 Mounting the drum module

Use the provided hardware in order to secure and mount the drum module. This will usually be placed above or to the left of the hi-hat.

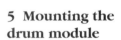

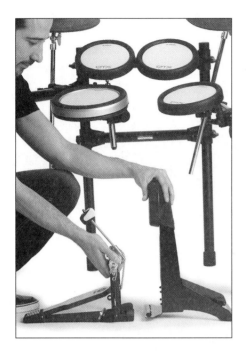

6 Setting the bass drum and hi-hat

Place the kit on a suitable mat to avoid slipping. Start with the bass drum pad, follow the instructions and securely set this pad so it will not move while you play. Then, attach the bass drum pedal to the pad. Continue with setting up the hi-hat stand and hi-hat cymbal pads. Use the provided hi-hat clutch to enable the pedal to control the opening of the hi-hat cymbals.

7 Connecting the leads

After you have re-checked the complete setup, you are ready to connect the leads. Every pad needs to be connected to its appropriate place on the drum module. Most kits will have this clearly labelled. If not, apply your own labelling (this will be very useful at a later stage).

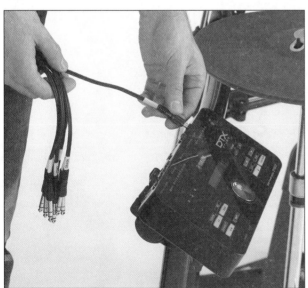

8 Connecting to a power source

After you are pleased with the setup and have secured all the leads, use the provided power lead to connect the drum module to the mains.

9 Connecting to an amplifier

Although your drum kit is assembled, it will not produce any sound if it is not connected to an amplifier. With the correct leads you can connect the drum module to any amplifier or sound system in order to hear your kit. Alternatively, you can connect a pair of headphones to the drum module and keep your neighbours happy.

The Drum Module

The drum module is the electronic brain that controls the drum and cymbal pads in the kit. All the sounds that you will be able to play are stored in this unit. Therefore, every pad will need to be connected to it with a jack cable. The module also connects to the amplifier, headphones, sound system, and any external audio device you want to use.

The drum module comes built-in with many sounds and often backing tracks as well. You may also be able to upload your own sounds to the module.

Each drum module should have a display that provides you with information and the ability to change factors within the general setup of the kit as well as each individual sound. The fundamental parameters you want to get familiar with as soon as possible are volume, drum kit selection, individual sound selection, using the mixer, and controlling the effects.

Volume
This refers to changing the general sound level of the kit. There will usually be a master volume button or dial that is easily visible. Check your drum module and ensure that you know exactly where it is.

Drum Kit Selection
Electronic drum kits come with many built-in sounds. These sounds are often combined by the manufacturer into stylistic drum kits. There will usually be a button (with arrows pointing up and down) or a dial that will enable you to change between kits. When you first start playing your electronic drum kit, you may wish to spend some time going through all the various drum sounds, and maybe make a note of which ones inspire you the most, so you can go back to them in the future when playing the kit.

Using the Mixer
Your kit may have individual sliders that enable you to change the volume of sounds within the kit. For example, if you are happy with the kit you are using but feel that the snare drum should be louder, push the slider up until you reach the desired dynamic level. It is best to use this sporadically and aim to make these adjustments with your playing rather than with the mixer, as this will make you a more sensitive and musical drummer.

Individual Sound Selection
Although the manufacturer grouped many sounds into kits, there are always additional sounds that can be integrated into your own custom setups. You can also take an existing drum kit and change one or more sounds within it to fit your musical taste. The process of changing individual sounds is mostly straightforward but different for each kit. Check the manufacturer's manual to understand how to do this with your kit.

Controlling the Effects
This refers to the overall setup as well as individual sounds. There are many parameters (reverb, stereo panning etc.) to each electronic sound that can be changed according to your musical tastes. Do not worry about this too much at the early stages, but if you feel curious try changing these parameters until you understand what each one does to the sound. This will help you achieve your own individual sound.

Posture

When setting up your kit, make sure everything is within easy reach. Sit upright, maintain a balanced and relaxed posture, and ensure that your shoulders are relaxed.

Do not set the cymbal stands too high or have the toms at angles which are impossible to play.

The top rim of the snare drum should be approximately waist high when you are seated.

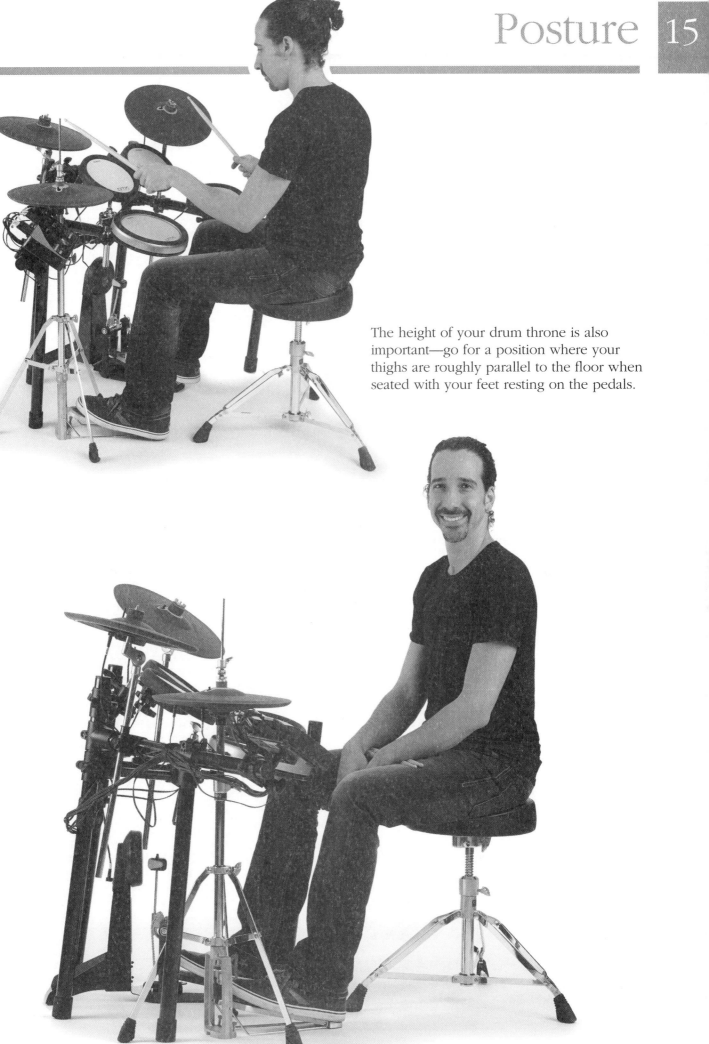

The height of your drum throne is also important—go for a position where your thighs are roughly parallel to the floor when seated with your feet resting on the pedals.

Sticks and Stick Control

Sticks

Drumsticks come in many shapes and sizes, so choose a pair that feels comfortable to you. As a suggestion, start with a medium pair of sticks made of hickory or maple, then make adjustments as needed.

Choose your drumstick from a reputable brand and ensure that the sticks are straight. This is easily checked by rolling the stick on a flat surface— if it wobbles it means it is warped, so look for another pair.

There are different sticks that mainly offer lower dynamic levels, but since volume can easily be adjusted with an electronic kit, choose a wooden stick, at least at first, to help you develop good stick control.

You should avoid nylon-tipped sticks, as these could mark the surface of rubber pads. If you wish to use brushes, nylon brushes are best, and only on mesh heads.

Tip

Tap the sticks on the counter and listen to their pitch — try to pick a pair with the same pitch, which means the wood is the same weight and density.

Stick Control

There are two basic ways of holding the sticks:

- **Matched grip**, where both sticks are held in the same overhand way. Most contemporary drummers favour the matched grip for power and speed.

- **Traditional grip**, where the left hand holds the stick from underneath. The right-hand grip is an overhand (matched) grip.

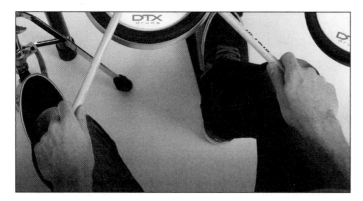

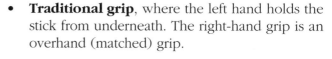

Matched Grip

With the palm of your right hand facing down, hold the stick about one third of the distance from the butt end so it pivots between the thumb and joint of the first finger. Your thumbnail should point straight down the shaft towards the tip. Follow the same concept to achieve consistent grip with your left hand.

Traditional Grip

With your left palm facing up, let your first finger curl around the stick, then bring your second, third and fourth fingers gently around onto the stick to guide and stabilise it. The right-hand position is the same as for the matched grip. Remember reliable stick control is achieved by a solid grip which is relaxed.

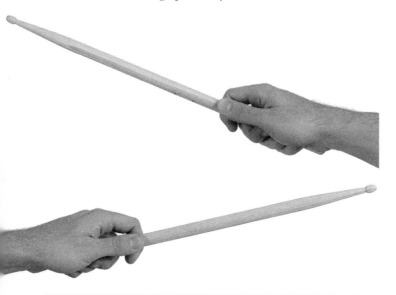

The Stroke

The first step in developing technique is to learn the stroke. Keep your arms fairly steady, moving the sticks mainly from the wrists. Too much arm motion can create a strain in the muscles, hampering your ability to play with speed and control. Follow these steps and practise slowly every day in order to develop a solid stroke:

- Hold both sticks about ten inches above the snare drum head. Keep your arms relaxed and slightly away from your body.

- With a snappy and relaxed motion, drop the tip end of the right stick to the centre of the head and allow it to rebound back to the starting position.
- Repeat steps one and two with your left stick. Keep practising this stroke, alternating the hands.
- As you relax you will feel the natural bounce of the stick doing most of the work. Try to obtain the same sound from both sticks.

The Bass Drum

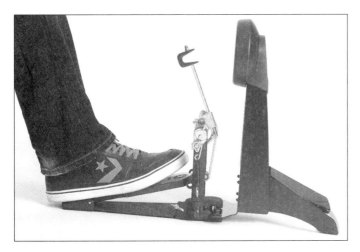 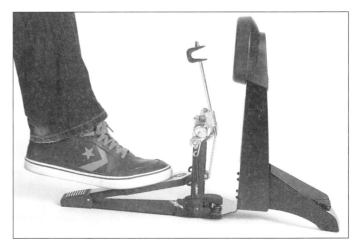

There are two basic ways of playing the bass drum pedal. One way is to have the whole foot flat on the pedal. This is referred to as the 'heel-down technique'. This technique is mainly used when playing softer types of music such as jazz.

The other way of playing the bass drum pedal is to raise the heel of your foot so that only your toes are touching the pedal. This uses larger muscles and transfers more force to the pedals and is used for heavier styles of music such as rock and metal. Logically this technique is called 'heel-up'. Many drummers find this technique most effective if the toes are only half way up the pedal and not all the way at the top. Experiment and see what works the best for you.

Sometimes a combination of both methods is used. Try both ways to see which is most comfortable for you. Ideally, you want to be able to use both and choose the one that is most suitable for the music played.

Adjust the tension spring on your bass drum pedal so that there is just enough tension to move the beater onto the head of the drum when you rest your foot on the pedal. Minor adjustments to this tension can make playing the pedal much easier, so take the time to experiment and find the most suitable position according to your technique.

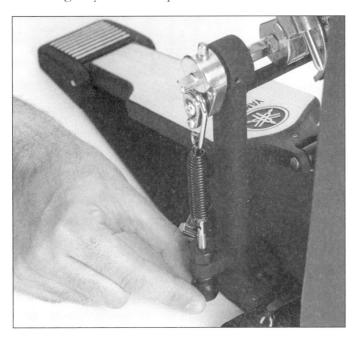 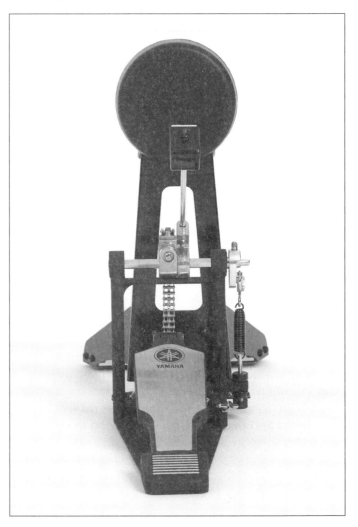

Your electronic hi-hat can either have one or two cymbals. If your electronic hi-hat came with two cymbals simply set it up as you would do with an acoustic hi-hat i.e. position the bottom cymbal six to ten inches above the top rim of the snare. Adjust the clutch to secure the top cymbal so that the felts touch the cymbal without choking it. Position the cymbals so that they are 0.5" to 1.5" apart and ensure that you are comfortable playing it.

If your electronic hi-hat only includes one cymbal (like the one used in this book) the set up will slightly differ, but you will be able to achieve the same functionality. After setting the hi-hat stand, secure the cymbal with the provided clutch and place it on the stand. Make final height adjustments so that the hi-hat is placed in a position comfortable for you.

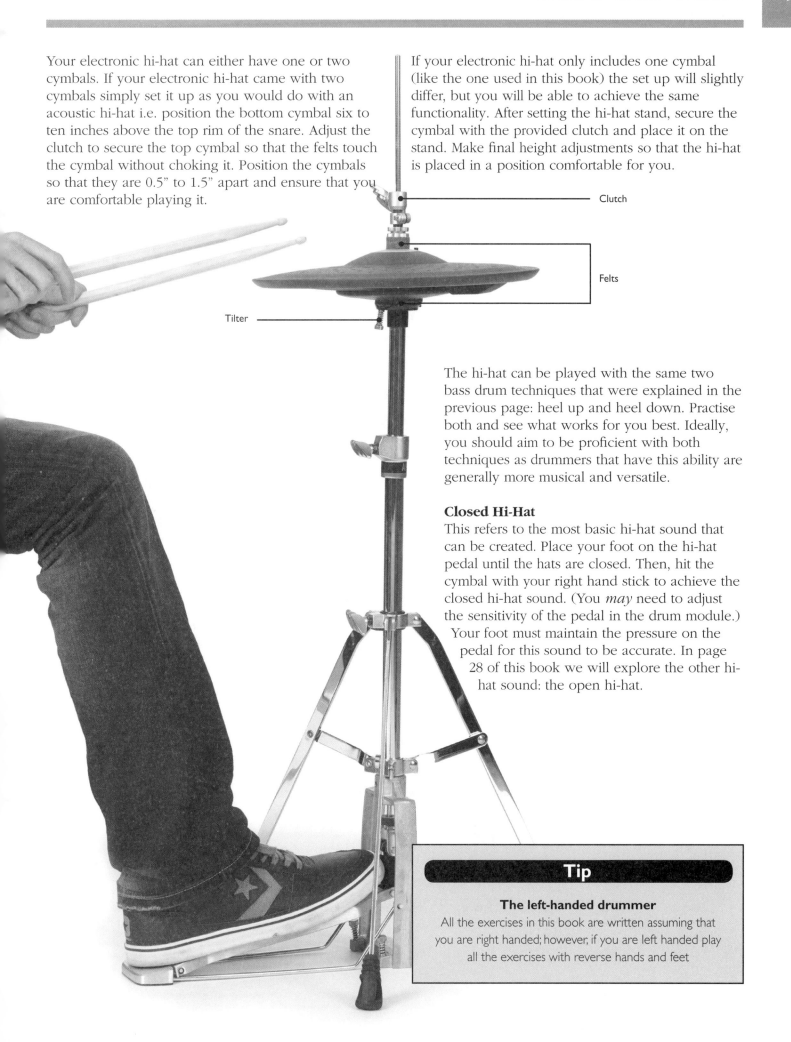

Clutch

Felts

Tilter

The hi-hat can be played with the same two bass drum techniques that were explained in the previous page: heel up and heel down. Practise both and see what works for you best. Ideally, you should aim to be proficient with both techniques as drummers that have this ability are generally more musical and versatile.

Closed Hi-Hat
This refers to the most basic hi-hat sound that can be created. Place your foot on the hi-hat pedal until the hats are closed. Then, hit the cymbal with your right hand stick to achieve the closed hi-hat sound. (You *may* need to adjust the sensitivity of the pedal in the drum module.) Your foot must maintain the pressure on the pedal for this sound to be accurate. In page 28 of this book we will explore the other hi-hat sound: the open hi-hat.

Tip

The left-handed drummer
All the exercises in this book are written assuming that you are right handed; however, if you are left handed play all the exercises with reverse hands and feet

Notation

Reading music is easy. Once you understand the fundamentals, you will take to it in no time. Drum music is written on five parallel lines called a *stave*.

Each drum is written on a different line on the stave, as shown below. The notation for electronic drums is exactly the same as acoustic drums.

Hi-hat (w/sticks)   Hi-hat (w/foot)   Crash cymbal   Snare   Hi tom   Mid tom   Floor tom   Bass drum   Ride cymbal

Rhythmic Notation

Music is divided into **measures**, which are separated by **barlines**. Double barlines show the end of a section, and **final barlines** mark the end of the tune.

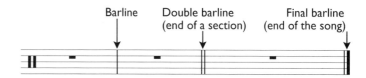

A note's **rhythmic value** is determined by its shape, stem, and flag: Whole notes (o) equal four beats and are counted 1-2-3-4. Half notes (♩) equal two beats, and two half notes equal one whole note. A quarter note (♩) equals one beat. Two quarter notes equal a half note and four quarter notes equal a whole note.

An eighth note (♪) is equal to half a beat. Two eighth notes equal a quarter note, four eighth notes equal a half note, and eight eighth notes equal a whole note.

Eighth notes are counted with "+" or as "ands" (1+2+3+4+), and can be grouped together by beams.

For each note there is an equivalent **rest**. A rest is a period of silence that takes the place of a note.

For example, a quarter-note rest equals one beat of silence.

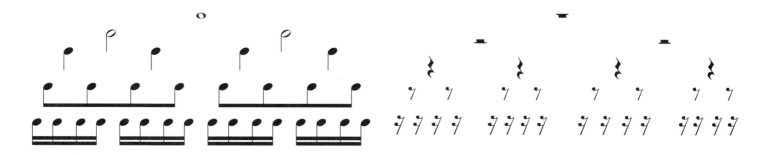

Counting Time

A **metronome** is a device that keeps regular beat, or *pulse*. This will be very helpful when practising and will help to develop a good sense of time.

The metronome can be adjusted to play at many speeds and rhythms. Speed is measured in beats per minute, abbreviated as BPM. Acoustic drummers have to purchase a metronome separately or use an app on their phone or tablet, but most electronic drum kits come with a built-in metronome. Ensure that you know how to access the metronome in your kit and are able to use it with ease.

In the first example you will need to concentrate on counting.

Track 1 is written in common time (or 4/4), so you will hear a four beat count at the start. Keep the hi-hat closed with your left foot on the pedal and play the crotchet (quarter note) closed hi-hat pattern with your right hand.

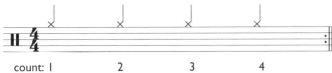

count: 1   2   3   4

Count 1, 2, 3, 4 throughout the track, making sure that each count coincides exactly with each strike of the hi-hat. If you get out of time with the music, stop and start again from the beginning.

Keeping good time means not speeding up or slowing down. This is especially important for the drummer. You may have greatest rhythms and fills in the world, but if you can't play in time you will never be popular with your fellow musicians.

To develop a good sense of time, practise all the exercises with the audio tracks and with a metronome.

Try playing each exercise at different tempos, from slow to fast. Never speed up or slow down gradually (unless specified) – keep a steady beat throughout. Always take a short break before trying an exercise at a new tempo.

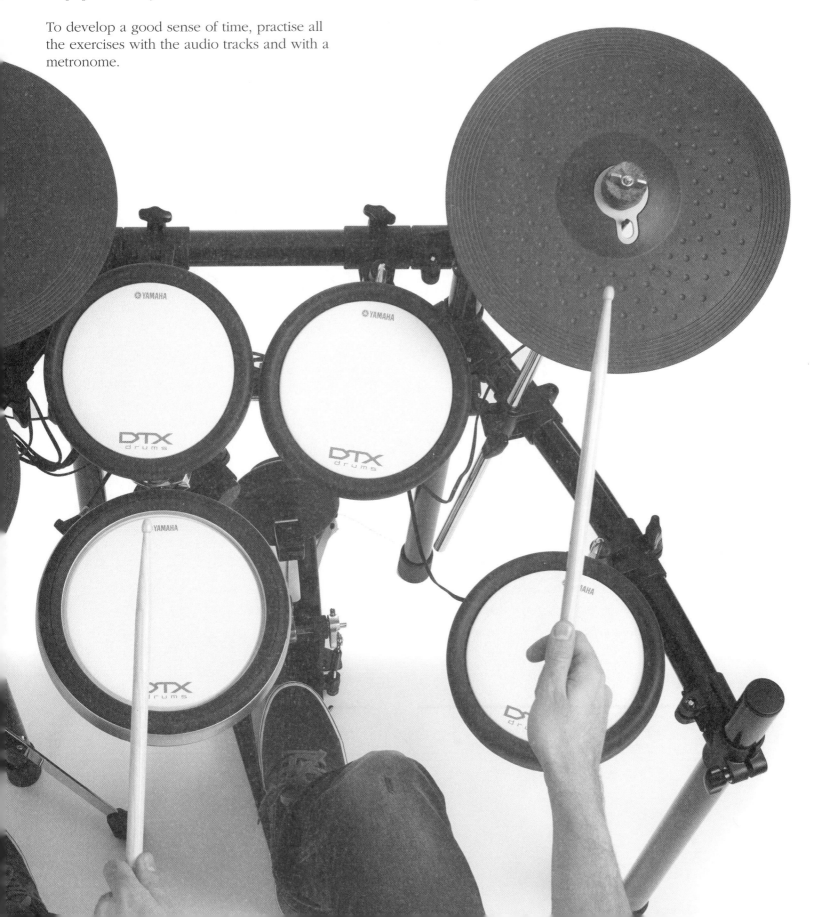

Basic Rock Rhythms

Now let's try playing a basic rock rhythm. We'll break it down into three stages:

Stage 1
Play the following eighth note (or quaver) rhythm on the closed hi-hat with your right hand.
Say the count as you play: 1 + 2 + 3 + 4 + etc.
Keep practising this exercise until you can play it with smoothness and ease.

 Track 2 demonstrates this rhythm slowly, and

 Track 3 demonstrates it slightly faster.

Exercise 1

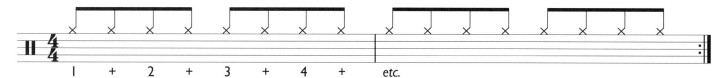

Stage 2
Play the hi-hat rhythm as before, but now also play the snare drum with your left hand on beats 2 and 4. This means that on beats 2 and 4 you are playing both the snare and hi-hat simultaneously. If you have trouble putting the snare and hi-hat parts together, isolate the snare part and just play on beats 2 & 4. Once you've got that rock steady, add the eighth note hi-hat part.

 Track 4 demonstrates this slowly, and

 Track 5 demonstrates it slightly faster.

Exercise 2

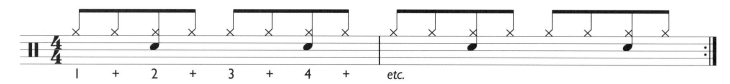

Stage 3
Play the bass drum with your right foot on beats 1 and 3. When playing the bass and snare parts, make sure every beat falls exactly in time with the hi-hat pattern. And don't forget to keep counting!

 Listen to **Track 6** to hear how this should sound.

Exercise 3

When playing the closed hi-hat and snare drum your right hand crosses over your left hand as shown here.

Extending the Beat

Having practised the basic rock rhythm on its own, let's extend it slightly.

Have a look through the example below, which lasts for nine bars. The first four bars are repeated; this equals eight counts of four, then in the ninth bar you'll end on a hi-hat cymbal and bass drum on beat 1.

Track 7 Exercise 4

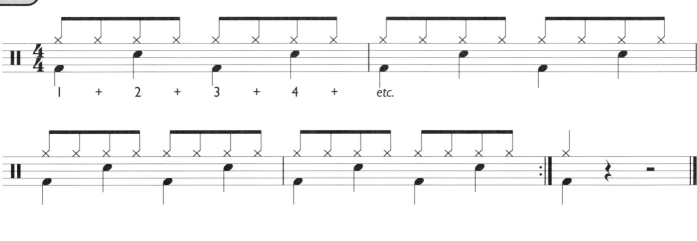

The crash cymbal is often used to highlight the beginning of a phrase or accent certain musical figures. It's normally the cymbal placed nearest the hi-hats.

To play the crash, strike the edge of the cymbal with the shoulder or shaft of the drum stick, using your normal grip.

Now try this repeated four-bar phrase, a variation on the previous track, which features the crash cymbal on beat one of bars 1, 3, 5, 7 and 9 – listen to **Track 8** to hear a demonstration.

Don't forget to keep counting as you play!

Track 8 Exercise 5

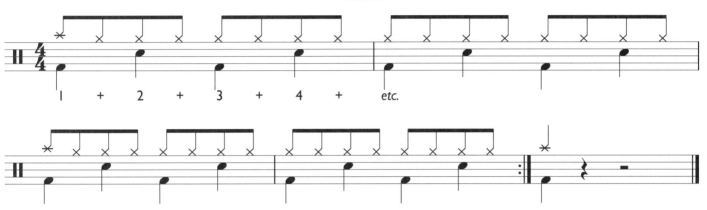

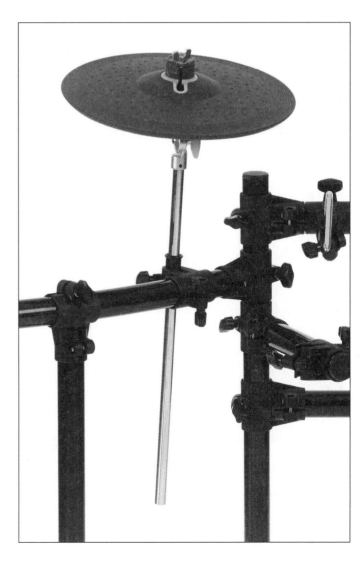

Tip

Placing the Crash cymbal

It may take you a while to decide how high you wish to place your crash and also your ride. Check out other drummers, and see how high, or how low they have theirs. It is important that you shouldn't be straining or stretching too far to play them.

The Open Hi-Hat

By now you should feel comfortable playing the closed hi-hat. In this exercise we will introduce the *open* hi-hat sound. This sound is creating by slightly loosening the pressure of the hi-hat foot pedal. Aim to master an efficient movement and only loosen the foot pedal as much as needed to produce the open hi-hat sound.

As mentioned previously, most electronic hi-hats will only have one 'hat' as such; however the overall effect is still the same, as whenever the pedal is released, the open sound is achieved. Remember to always keep your foot in contact with the pedal and practise the two techniques mentioned previously on page 18.

Hi-hat played with the heel-up technique

Hi-hat played with the heel-down technique

In the example below we have a two-bar hi-hat pattern. The '+' shows us when the hi-hat should be closed, and the 'o' shows us when it should be open.

Remember that the timing of the opening and closing must accurately reflect the notation. Practise this with a metronome until it feels comfortable and ensure that your posture remains stable throughout.

Track 9 Exercise 6

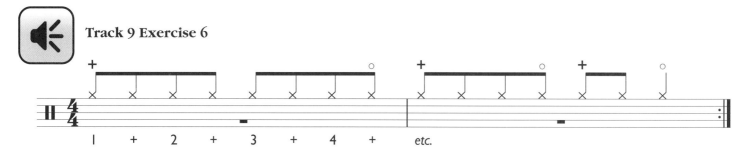

When playing the ride cymbal, strike the cymbal with the tip of the stick, about halfway between the bell and the outer edge. Let the stick rebound after every beat.

In most grooves the ride cymbal can be an alternative to the hi-hat. Let's play the track we learnt on page 27 with the ride cymbal as our leading voice. The bass drum, snare drum, and crash cymbal patterns will be exactly the same as before.

Track 10 Exercise 7

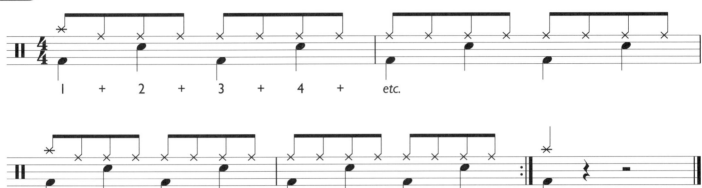

Grooves: Rock

In this lesson we will learn how to play rock grooves by using everything we have learnt so far. Drum grooves from different styles can be similar, so you will be able to use many of the same grooves in many different styles of music. However, the main focus in this early stage is to learn how to coordinate the limbs effectively with good time.

The groove pages should be practised daily until you feel comfortable with playing them at various speeds. You can play the grooves with the backing tracks that are provided with this book or you could play along with your favourite music.

Track 11 Exercise 8

Track 12 Exercise 9

Track 13 Exercise 10

Track 14 Exercise 11

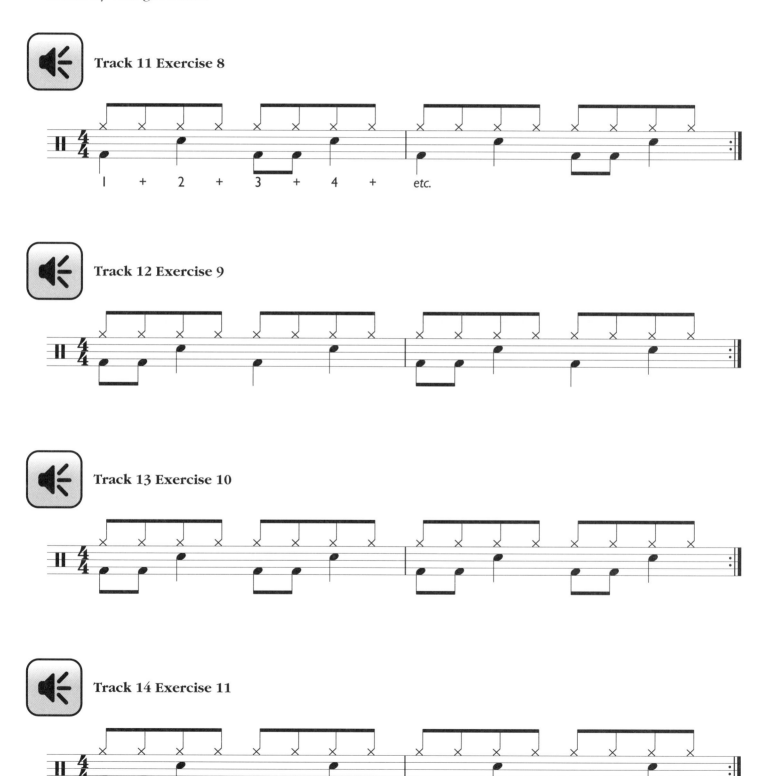

The following four examples are two-bar grooves. This means that the groove will be slightly different in each bar so you need to be able to adapt quickly. The process of reading notation and translating it onto the drum kit takes time to develop. Therefore, practise and progress through this book at your own pace.

The more time you spend on getting the foundation right, the better chance you have of developing further with your drumming.

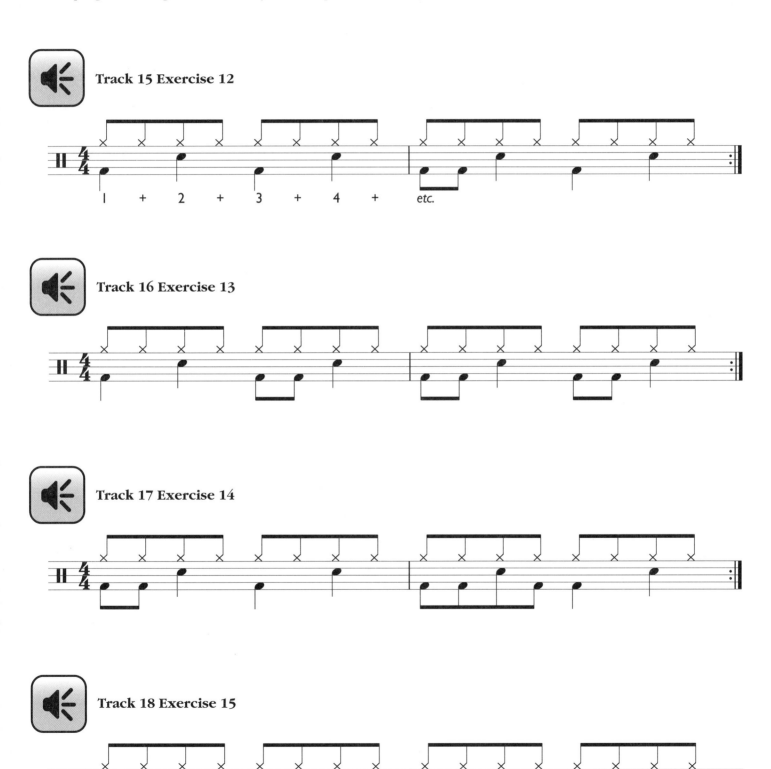

Track 15 Exercise 12

Track 16 Exercise 13

Track 17 Exercise 14

Track 18 Exercise 15

Grooves: Hip Hop

The hip hop grooves below are slightly more complex than the rock grooves you learnt previously. They will still only include the bass drum, snare, and consistent eighth notes on the hi-hat.

Practise these with the same ethos used in the rock chapter and aim to reach a stage where you can play these grooves with your favourite hip hop music or the provided backing tracks.

 **Track 19 Exercise 16**

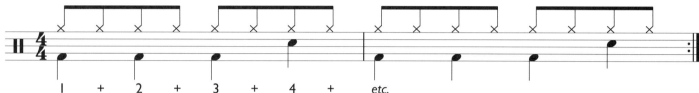

 Track 20 Exercise 17

 Track 21 Exercise 18

 Track 22 Exercise 19

Now let's try two-bar hip hop grooves. This time we'll also add the open hi-hat sound that was explained on page 28.

Focus on the timing of opening and closing the hi-hat and ensure that the consistency of the groove is not affected.

Track 23 Exercise 20

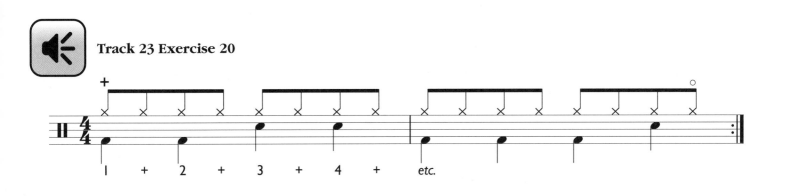

Track 24 Exercise 21

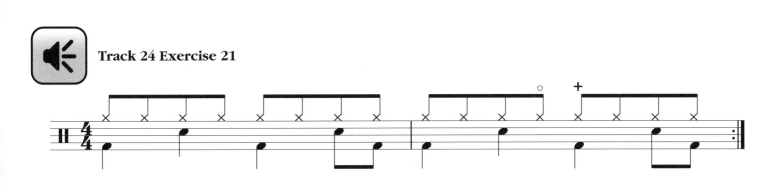

Track 25 Exercise 22

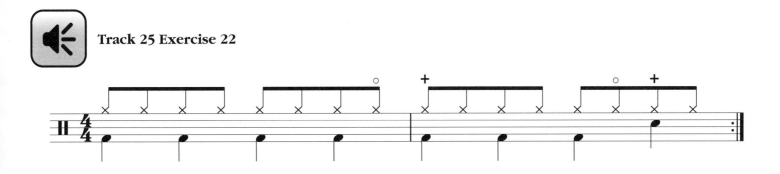

Track 26 Exercise 23

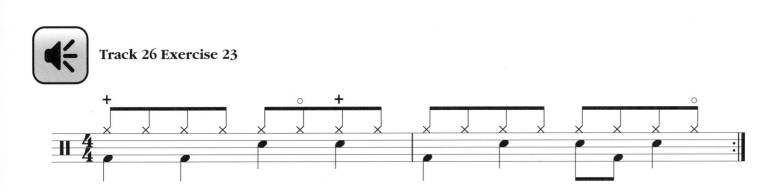

Grooves: Funk

In this lesson we will explore a new style: funk. The funk grooves presented on this page include a new symbol, the eighth-note rest ⁊. This represents a rest of half a beat.

Counting the eighth notes throughout and understanding where not to play is the key for these grooves.

 Track 27 Exercise 24

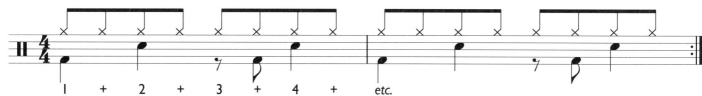

 Track 28 Exercise 25

 Track 29 Exercise 26

 Track 30 Exercise 27

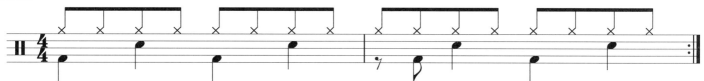

The two-bar grooves below are in the funk style and include the eighth-note rest we learnt in the previous page. Playing on the '+', or the 'offbeats', as these are referred to in music, strengthens the natural feel of funk.

Practise these grooves with a metronome to ensure that you play the offbeat accurately. In examples 3 and 4 we will also add the open hi-hat and crash cymbal.

 Track 31 Exercise 28

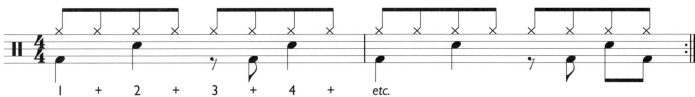

 Track 32 Exercise 29

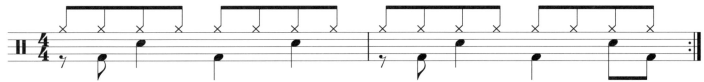

 Track 33 Exercise 30

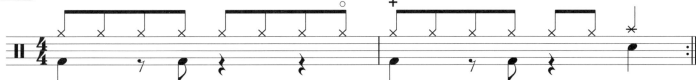

 Track 34 Exercise 31

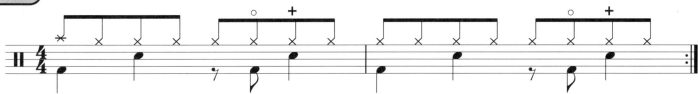

Grooves: Disco

There are two important techniques that are integral to disco drumming. We will practise these separately before attempting the disco two-bar grooves. Once you feel confident with these techniques, feel free to incorporate them into the other styles you have learnt.

Syncing the Bass Drum and Snare Backbeat

The first technique involves playing the bass drum and snare together. Most drummers find this very challenging at first, therefore it requires special attention. The natural tendency will be to play the one of the voices slightly earlier than the other.

Your focus should be to achieve perfect sync between the drum voices. In disco drumming, the bass drum will generally be playing on every quarter note (also known as 'four on the floor') and the snare on beats 2 and 4. In popular music beats 2 and 4 are often referred to as the 'backbeat'.

Track 35 Exercise 32

Offbeat Hi-Hats

The second technique focuses on the hi-hat pattern and consists of playing only the offbeats. This means that there will always be a rest on the beat and hi-hat played on the offbeat.

The example below will help you develop this technique before attempting the full disco grooves on page 37.

Track 36 Exercise 33

The two-bar disco grooves below include everything that you have learnt until now, combining the two techniques which were detailed in the previous page. Adding the stylistic offbeat open hi-hat can be challenging at first, but with practice and perseverance you will be able to groove along to your favourite disco music in no time.

Focus on the timing of opening and closing the hi-hat, ensure that the other drum voices are consistent and your posture is not compromised (not leaning backwards or sideways). When you feel confident with these grooves, try playing them with the ride cymbal instead of the hi-hats.

Track 37 Exercise 34

Track 38 Exercise 35

Track 39 Exercise 36

Track 40 Exercise 37

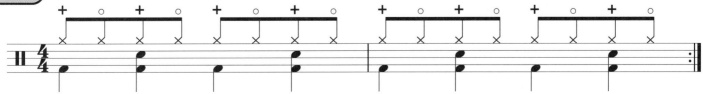

Drum Fills

Drum fills tend to signal the end of a phrase (often at the end of a chorus or verse) to break up the regularity of a beat, and to lead the way to a different part of a song. In order to explore drum fills we need to introduce another note called a sixteenth note (or semiquaver). It looks similar to the eighth note but has two tails instead of one 𝅘𝅥𝅮 .

When playing in 4/4 there are sixteen sixteenth notes to every bar. To count these notes we subdivide each beat into four parts and they are counted like this:

1 e & a, 2 e & a, 3 e & a, 4 e & a *etc.*

Here's your first chance to try some semiquavers. Count steadily as you play and make sure each count coincides with each beat played.

Start with both sticks at the same height above the drum and play this exercise using the technique as described in the stroke on page 17. **Track 41** lets you hear how it should sound.

 Track 41 Exercise 38

Double Stroke Sticking

In all the exercises so far you have been playing one beat with each hand – this is known as single stroke sticking: **R L R L** etc. For extra practice, you can play this exercise using double stroke sticking – playing two beats with each hand: **R R L L** etc.

Now add the bass drum and hi-hat parts to form the rhythm written out below. You will notice the bass drum falls on beats 1, 2, 3, 4 throughout, with the hi-hat falling on beats 2 and 4. Notice that the hi-hats are played with the foot, on the backbeat.

 Track 42 Exercise 39

Tip

This is an excellent exercise for building up speed and improving technique. If you want to concentrate more on this aspect of drumming, a book of drum Rudiments is highly recommended.

For extra practice play this exercise using double stroke sticking (as shown above the stave). Make sure your bass drum maintains a constant tempo while the snare part doubles up each bar, playing 4, 8, then 16 beats.

Listen to **Track 42**, and practise slowly until you can play along.

Now let's put these rhythms into context and create drum fills of one, two, three, and four beats. The examples below include a one-bar groove with a fill in the second bar. Play these repeatedly at various speeds until you feel confident.

Although the fills are notated on the snare drum, you can easily adapt these to be used around the kit by replacing any of the snare notes with toms.

 Track 43 Exercise 40

Rock

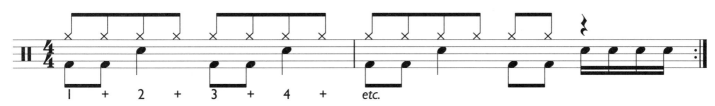

 Track 44 Exercise 41

Hip Hop

 Track 45 Exercise 42

Funk

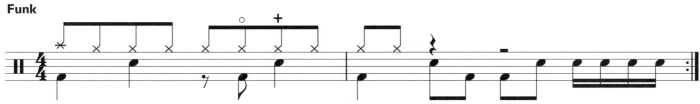

 Track 46 Exercise 43

Disco

Grooves: Metal

Metal drumming is very exciting, and even if you don't listen to much metal, you'll hopefully appreciate the way these stylistic grooves can stretch your abilities and enable you to use many of the skills you have acquired throughout this book. There are two integral techniques that are frequently used in metal drumming. Let's look at these in detail.

Leading with an Open Sound
This refers to playing the leading voice (open hi-hats or crash/ride cymbal) in a groove. Pay attention to the balance between the kit instruments.

The leading open sound should not be louder than the bass drum and snare. It is also important to ensure that your posture is not compromised in any way and you are able to change between hats and crash/ride fluently.

After you achieve this groove, try as an alternative to play the open hi-hats as quarter notes rather than eighth notes. This is very common in metal drumming but will also be extremely useful in other styles. If you want to challenge yourself go back and play all the grooves you have learnt with a quarter-note lead rather than an eighth-note.

Track 47 Exercise 44

Track 48 Exercise 45

Half-Time Feel

Half-time feel grooves have only one backbeat in each bar. It is placed on the third quarter note rather than on the usual backbeats on the second and fourth quarter notes (i.e., beat 3 instead of beats 2 and 4).

Combining the half-time concept with the leading open sound creates very convincing metal grooves.

You will notice that the rhythm of the leading voice in Example 2 is in quarter notes.

The two-bar metal grooves below combine many of the concepts introduced in this book. Practise slowly and build up speed, ensuring that your technique is accurate and balanced. When you feel ready, try playing the grooves with your favourite metal music.

Track 49 Exercise 46

Track 50 Exercise 47

Track 51 Exercise 48

Track 52 Exercise 49

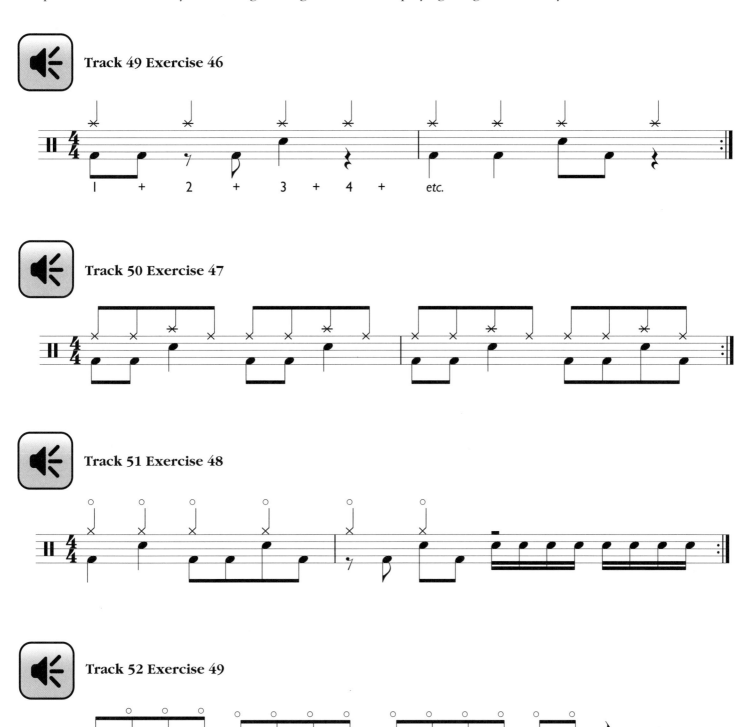

Changing Grooves

Another essential skill for every drummer is having the ability to change between grooves and styles fluently. Mostly, drummers will use fills between the changes. Over the next two pages we will practise four examples; each one consists of eight bars of music. We will use the styles that you have learnt as well as the techniques, fills, and a few extra stylistic tricks that will make your drumming sound more convincing overall.

Play each example repeatedly until you feel comfortable. Use a metronome or the track provided with this book in order to ensure that the pulse is consistent.

If you want to challenge yourself, practise moving between the examples without stopping. For this type of practice it will be best to use songs that you like in any style and aim to move between the examples with ease, until you feel confident to create your own grooves, variations and fills.

 Track 53 Exercise 50

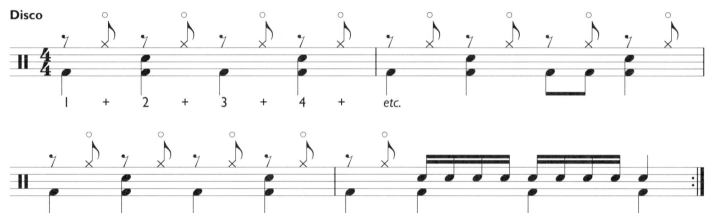

 Track 54 Exercise 51

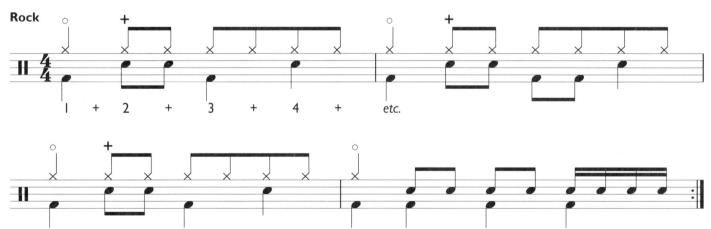

Track 55 Exercise 52

Funk

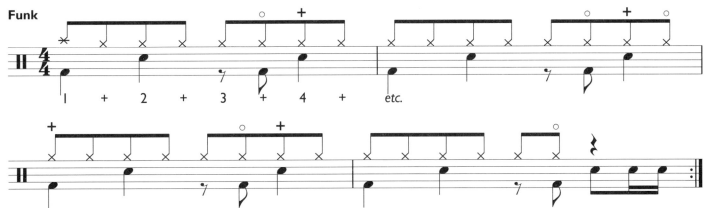

 Track 56 Exercise 53

Metal

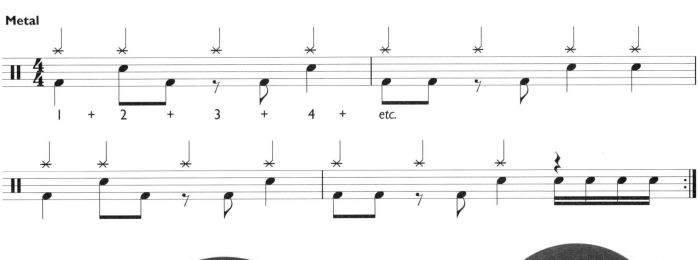

Performance Piece

Now it's time to put everything together and play a whole drumming piece. Feel free to practise this in sections first, and combine those as you feel more comfortable with the notation.

Try to make time to practise daily and aim to increase the speed until you are able to play along with conviction.

Tracks 57/58 Performance Piece Demonstration/Backing Track

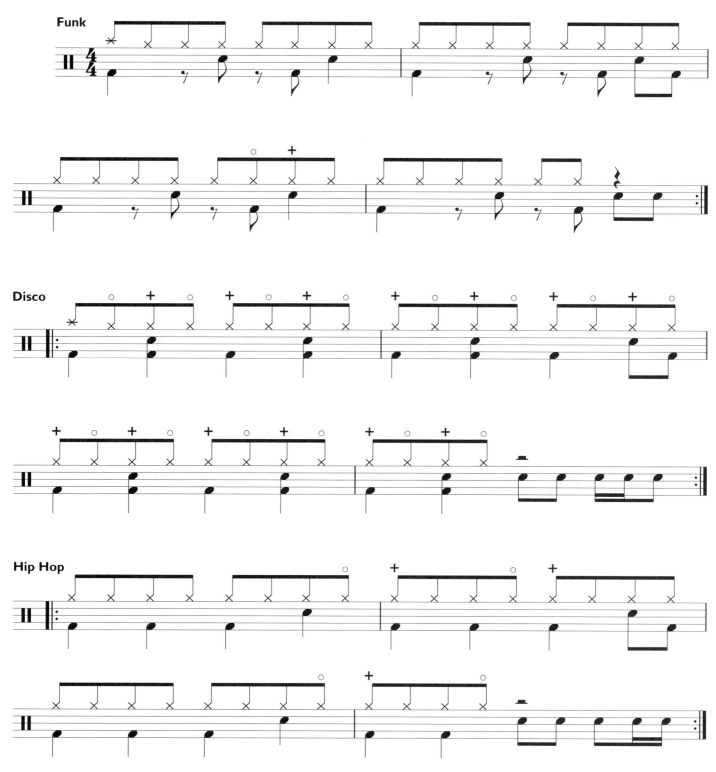

Metal

We've also created individual audio tracks of each style you can play along with. These last for about two minutes each, so feel free to start creating your own beats and fills along with the backing track when you've mastered each groove.

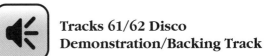
Tracks 59/60 Funk
Demonstration/Backing Track

Tracks 61/62 Disco
Demonstration/Backing Track

Tracks 63/64 Hip Hop
Demonstration/Backing Track

Tracks 65/66 Metal
Demonstration/Backing Track

Tracks 67/68 Rock
Demonstration/Backing Track
(see page 27 for notation)

Care and Maintenance

Maintaining your instrument and keeping it in good condition requires attention and care. Naturally, an electronic drum kit will demand less regular maintenance than an acoustic kit, but there are a few fundamentals aspects you must be aware of when owning an electronic kit.

Leads

The electronic drum kit has many leads. Most will be standard mono leads, but a few may be stereo leads. Consult your instructions from the manufacturer. These include leads that connect between the module and the pads, leads that connect the module to an electric source, and leads that connects the module to an external sound system or an amplifier. It is crucial that all leads are kept in good condition, so avoid having a 'lead spaghetti' by organising all your leads properly when initially setting up the kit. Whenever the kit is moved, ensure that all the parts are back to their original place and the leads are not tangled.

General Maintenance

Luckily, there is no need to change drumheads like an acoustic drum kit. However, it is important to keep the drum kit and especially the drum module and all exposed lead sockets clean. Cover the drum module with a piece of cloth whenever the kit is not played. This will help you avoid many of the most common problems that these types of kits can have.

Suggested Listening

Now you're armed with the techniques of how to play beats in a variety of styles, it's a good idea to familiarise yourself with some classic songs; all of these below are distinctive because of their beat. Listening and studying different drummers will help you develop your own distinctive sound.

Be My Baby The Ronettes (Hal Blaine)
Fifty Ways To Leave Your Lover Paul Simon
   (Steve Gadd)
I Can't Explain The Who (Keith Moon)
I Am The Resurrection The Stone Roses (Reni)
Tomorrow Never Knows The Beatles (Ringo Starr)
We Will Rock You Queen (Roger Taylor)
When The Levee Breaks Led Zeppelin
   (John Bonham)
White Room Cream (Ginger Baker)

If you're more interested in specifically electronic drummers, check out these players, some of which use either wholly electronic kits, or use aspects of electronic kits in their setups (either live or in the studio):

Tim Alexander (Primus)
Rick Allen (Def Leppard)
Rob Bourdon (Linkin Park)
Danny Carey (Tool)
Sly Dunbar (Black Uhuru)
Stephen Morris (New Order)
Neil Peart (Rush)
Damon Reece (Massive Attack)

Noam Lederman is a highly skilled drummer, composer, and author. Having graduated from the prestigious London Guildhall School of Music and Drama, he went on to create a successful music career combining performing, composing, and writing. Whilst playing with big bands, Noam was fortunate to play with renowned musicians such as Billy Cobham, Dave Liebman, and Kenny Wheeler. He then went on to work with top artists such as: Corinne Bailey Rae, State of Bengal, Mark Hill (producer), Trevor Horn (producer), and many others. Noam has taken part in many prominent UK and international music festivals such as Womad, Glastonbury, Reading, and Sonar, as well as appearing on MTV.

Throughout his career, Noam has recorded many studio albums, toured extensively across the globe, and has been involved with writing and developing over a hundred books and various music education methods. As Chief Examiner for international music board Rockschool, Noam developed and produced their highly successful 2012 syllabus.

Other works include the *Hot Rock* series for drums (Rockschool), *GCSE Performance Pieces - Drums* (Rhinegold Education), and more. Noam's collaboration with Music Sales has been consistent and fruitful over the years, producing popular play alongs such as Led Zeppelin and AC/DC, as well as the top apps *Killer Beats* and *Freestyle*.

For more information or if you wish to contact the author, please visit his website at **www.noamlederman.com**.